25 Invitations of Christmas
An Advent Devotional

DAVE STRADLING

The 25 Invitations of Christmas
Copyright © 2023 Dave Stradling

Cover Artist & Book Illustrations: Justin Lamperski
Editing: Debbie Emmitt
Author Photo: Cassady K Photography
Book Layout Design: Shabbir Hussain

Published by: 30 Foot Salmon Publishing

ISBN: 979-8-9893561-0-2

CONTENTS

Introduction

On December 1, we begin our annual Advent calendar tradition, counting down the days until Christmas. Last year it was a *Star Wars Lego* calendar for our son, Reece, while his sister, Kitt, had her *Elf on the Shelf North Pole Advent Train* calendar. For twenty-five days each year, they awake eager to discover what surprise their calendar will offer.

These calendars capture the spirit of Advent, a time of anticipation. It's a feeling clearly on display when I'm impatiently asked how much longer until the next numbered door can be opened.

Originating from Latin, "advent" means "arrival." From as early as the sixth century, the church has prepared to celebrate the arrival of Jesus, the Christ, by participating in a season known as Advent. The four Sundays before Christmas are set aside for this purpose.

During Advent, four candles are often prominently displayed, each week being devoted to one candle. These four candles symbolize the gifts Christ brings: hope, love, joy, and peace. (Some traditions include a fifth white candle symbolizing the light and purity of Christ.)

Since stumbling upon the rich history of Advent in my mid-twenties, I've been a loyal fan. As I continued to dive deeper into Advent, I began noticing there are two ways we can wait for the arrival of Jesus. We can be passive in our waiting, or we can be active. Passive waiting virtually ensures we miss out on the gifts Christ brings while active waiting makes room within ourselves to receive these gifts. My guess is you're like me and can use all the hope, love, joy, and peace you can get!

As a way to count down to Christmas and actively wait for the arrival of Jesus, I have created this Advent calendar. Each day will offer a surprise: a fresh invitation for us to open. We'll walk together through the birth stories of Jesus, paying attention to where we are being offered opportunities to join in.

For me, this is the best way to read these stories. Not as an event that happened in the past, but as something that's happening right now. An event we can notice, step into, and participate in today. If we view the story of God being born into our world as nothing more than an event that happened 2,000 years ago, we might miss the Spirit that's still birthing hope, love, joy, and peace into our world today.

This Advent season, I hope you'll join me. And as you step into these twenty-five invitations of Christmas, may you be filled with more of the hope, love, joy, and peace that Christ brings.

Day 1

MAKING SPACE

READING: Luke 1:26–38

In the sixth month of Elizabeth's pregnancy, God sent the angel Gabriel to Nazareth, a town in Galilee, to a virgin pledged to be married to a man named Joseph, a descendant of David. The virgin's name was Mary. The angel went to her and said, "Greetings, you who are highly favored! The Lord is with you."

Mary was greatly troubled at his words and wondered what kind of greeting this might be. But the angel said to her, "Do not be afraid, Mary; you have found favor with God. You will conceive and give birth to a son, and you are to call him Jesus. He will be great and will be called the Son of the Most High. The Lord God will give him the throne of his father David, and he will reign over Jacob's descendants forever; his kingdom will never end."

"How will this be," Mary asked the angel, "since I am a virgin?"

The angel answered, "The Holy Spirit will come on you, and the power of the Most High will overshadow you. So the holy one to be born will be called the Son of God. Even Elizabeth your relative is going to have a child in her old age, and she who was said to be unable to conceive is in her sixth month. For no word from God will ever fail."

"I am the Lord's servant," Mary answered. "May your word to me be fulfilled." Then the angel left her.

There's an ancient parable about a teacher whose wisdom was known far and wide. Many would travel long distances to seek his counsel and learn from him.

One day, an important man came to see the teacher. He was a leader, used to commanding others and getting his way. Upon arrival, he was ushered into the teacher's room where he was asked the reason for his visit.

"I want you to teach me your wisdom," replied the man.

The teacher gave a knowing smile and suggested they first share tea. Once a fresh pot of steaming tea had been brought into the room, the teacher handed the man a cup and proceeded to pour the tea. Holding the cup in his hands, the man watched as the tea reached the rim.

"Stop!" he yelled as the burning tea spilled onto his lap. "Can't you see the cup is already full?"

"Yes," said the teacher. "This cup is like your mind. It's so full that nothing else will fit. Return to me with an empty cup."

As we begin our journey through Advent, we, like the man, must make space within ourselves to receive.

Think for a moment about what fills your mind.

If you're like me, a mental list probably forms immediately of all the responsibilities you carry. Maybe just the thought of that list raises your blood pressure. I get it.

And now with the Christmas season upon us, that list can often feel even more daunting. There's shopping to be done, parties to attend, ugly sweaters to buy, cookies to bake—the list goes on and on. How will we fit it all in?!

The problem with this way of living—bouncing around from one task to the next, creating little, if any, margin to breathe—is that our lives start looking like that overflowing teacup. There's so much filling our lives that we don't have time to fully receive the good that's coming our way. Sometimes we're trying to cram so much in, we aren't even aware of the good that's right in front of us. We're onto the next thing before we've had a chance to appreciate the gifts present in the moment.

So, we need a period when we slow down and leave a little space. Which, I know, sounds near impossible given the current season. But what if we did find a way to empty our cup, even a little? What if we were to create some space within our lives so we could receive the gifts this season promises: hope, love, joy, and peace? Wouldn't it be worth it if we walked away from Advent with a little more peace in our lives? Or a little more hope for the situation we're walking through?

I love the story Luke tells about Mary when she was first told she would give birth to the Messiah, Jesus. When she hears the news, she's shocked. Why is this happening to me? Why have I been chosen? And how is this even possible?

By the end of the conversation, she's all in. She's considered what it will require of her, and she's ready. Like any pregnancy, there's a sacrifice involved. She has to make space within herself as she allows her body to be borrowed for nine months.

But she thinks the sacrifice is worth it. She sees this opportunity as a gift and is willing to make space within herself for this child.

What would it look like to create some space in your life over these next twenty-five days? Is there something you can go without for a season? Is there something on your list that can be set aside so you don't miss any of the hope, love, joy, and peace that's being offered to you this Advent season?

INVITATION

FIND TIME EACH DAY TO BE AN
ACTIVE PARTICIPANT IN ADVENT.
SIT WITH THE STORY OF CHRISTMAS
AND LISTEN FOR HOW THE SPIRIT IS
BIRTHING HOPE, LOVE, JOY, AND PEACE
WITHIN YOU THIS SEASON.

SPACE FOR REFLECTION

- How can you make space each day to sit with the story of Christmas?

  _____

  _____

  _____

  _____

  _____

- Of the four gifts of Advent (hope, love, joy, and peace), which do you find yourself most in need of this year?

  _____

  _____

  _____

  _____

  _____

Day 2

AN INVITATION TO HOPE AGAIN

READING: John 1:1–14

In the beginning was the Word, and the Word was with God, and the Word was God. He was with God in the beginning. Through him all things were made; without him nothing was made that has been made. In him was life, and that life was the light of all mankind. The light shines in the darkness, and the darkness has not overcome it.

There was a man sent from God whose name was John. He came as a witness to testify concerning that light, so that through him all might believe. He himself was not the light; he came only as a witness to the light.

The true light that gives light to everyone was coming into the world. He was in the world, and though the world was made through him, the world did not recognize him. He came to that which was his own, but his own did not receive him. Yet to all who did receive him, to those who believed in his name, he gave the right to become children of God—children born not of natural descent, nor of human decision or a husband's will, but born of God.

The Word became flesh and made his dwelling among us. We have seen his glory, the glory of the one and only Son, who came from the Father, full of grace and truth.

While doing home renovations, we discovered a large number of mice were finding their way into our crawlspace. To solve this problem, we had to go around the entire foundation and seal any cracks. Mice can squeeze through a crack the size of a dime, or even the width of a pencil, so the sealing had to be thorough. After the initial sealing, we were still catching mice. My friend offered a suggestion for discovering any spaces we'd overlooked. Go into the crawlspace on a bright, sunny day and turn off all the lights. While in the darkness, he said, look for signs of daylight. That's where the mice would be getting in.

The next day, I did just that. Alone in the dark crawlspace, I scanned the perimeter for signs of light. As I looked around, I found daylight. There were my cracks.

The Gospel of John doesn't include the traditional Christmas story, but it does have its own riff on the birth of Jesus. In the story, there's this line: "The light shines in the darkness…" (John 1:4).

John doesn't explain what this darkness is. He doesn't try to rationalize it. For him, it's an assumed reality. In this world, there's darkness.

We all know this to be true. Turn on the news and you'll see it. Look at your own life and you'll recognize moments of darkness. We all have these experiences when it feels as if any semblance of light or hope are nonexistent.

When we find ourselves in such moments, it can be easy to focus on nothing but the darkness: all that's going wrong in our lives or the world around us. But John tells us the story doesn't end with darkness. Because in the darkness emerges a light. Yes, that light can often seem faint. It can feel far away. But, the truth of Christmas is that light is here.

This Advent, I want to offer you a way to regain any hope you might have lost this past year. Like me in the crawlspace scanning for signs of light, let's be intentional about looking for signs of light in our lives.

Whenever you come across something that sparks the flame of hope within you, write it down. Take a picture. Make a note in your phone. It can be as small as the first conscious breath you take in the morning, the sun shining on your face, or a text from a friend. Capture those moments. We'll call these our hope sightings.

By the end of Advent, I'd love for us to have a collection of hope sightings showing all the slivers of daylight shining through the cracks into our lives. Yes, the darkness won't be gone completely. But, this season, let's focus our attention on the light we experience. After all, that which we give attention to is what grows.

INVITATION

CAPTURE YOUR HOPE SIGHTINGS—
ALL THE MOMENTS THAT REVEAL
LIGHT AND HOPE.

SPACE FOR REFLECTION

Use the space below to begin listing your hope sightings.

1. ....
   ....
   ....

2. ....
   ....
   ....

3. ....
   ....
   ....

4. ....
   ....
   ....

5.

6.

7.

8.

9.

10.

Day
3

EMBRACING YOUR WHOLE STORY

READING: Matthew 1:1–18

This is the genealogy of Jesus the Messiah the son of David, the son of Abraham:

Abraham was the father of Isaac,
Isaac the father of Jacob,
Jacob the father of Judah and his brothers,
Judah the father of Perez and Zerah, whose mother was Tamar,
Perez the father of Hezron,
Hezron the father of Ram,
Ram the father of Amminadab,
Amminadab the father of Nahshon,
Nahshon the father of Salmon,
Salmon the father of Boaz, whose mother was Rahab,
Boaz the father of Obed, whose mother was Ruth,
Obed the father of Jesse,
and Jesse the father of King David.

David was the father of Solomon, whose mother
had been Uriah's wife,
Solomon the father of Rehoboam,
Rehoboam the father of Abijah,
Abijah the father of Asa,
Asa the father of Jehoshaphat,
Jehoshaphat the father of Jehoram,
Jehoram the father of Uzziah,
Uzziah the father of Jotham,
Jotham the father of Ahaz,
Ahaz the father of Hezekiah,
Hezekiah the father of Manasseh,
Manasseh the father of Amon,
Amon the father of Josiah,
and Josiah the father of Jeconiah and his brothers
at the time of the exile to Babylon.

After the exile to Babylon:
Jeconiah was the father of Shealtiel,
Shealtiel the father of Zerubbabel,
Zerubbabel the father of Abihud,
Abihud the father of Eliakim,
Eliakim the father of Azor,
Azor the father of Zadok,
Zadok the father of Akim,
Akim the father of Elihud,
Elihud the father of Eleazar,
Eleazar the father of Matthan,
Matthan the father of Jacob,
and Jacob the father of Joseph, the husband of
Mary, and Mary was the mother of Jesus who is
called the Messiah.

Thus there were fourteen generations in all from Abraham to David, fourteen from David to the exile to Babylon, and fourteen from the exile to the Messiah.

This is how the birth of Jesus the Messiah came about...

Before we even get to the birth of Jesus, Matthew starts us off with a genealogy. By today's standards, this isn't a great way to begin a story, especially one with such significance. Yet, Matthew finds it necessary to start the story of Jesus with a record of past generations.

As we read through the genealogy, there are plenty of names that make sense. Of course the Messiah would come from this heritage! But then, we come across names we wouldn't have expected to make the cut. Try googling "Manasseh." These are the relatives we keep off the guest list. The uncle we don't want our friends to meet.

Then there are the women. Besides Mary, the inclusion of women appears odd for a first-century document. Even more bizarre is how Bathsheba is introduced. Instead of being mentioned by name, she is described as "Uriah's wife." That odd description seems to be

Matthew's way of drawing our attention to the story of David, Bathsheba, and Uriah. But why bring up a story of adultery and murder? Why give extra attention to a story that seems best omitted from the genealogy of Jesus, the Messiah?

By including all these names and stories, we are being offered permission to own the entirety of our stories. If Christ, God in the flesh, can be birthed through a past as flawed as this one, there's hope for us.

When I was in high school, my band, 30 Foot Salmon, performed a song at our church's Christmas show. In every way, the performance was a disaster. Thirty seconds in, we all stopped and looked at each other. I told the crowd that was our dress rehearsal, and we were now ready to rock their world. Not a chance. Our second try was just as dismal as the first. We stopped the song midway and walked off stage, hiding in a locked room the rest of the night, too embarrassed to show our faces.

We all have moments in our past that we proudly display for the world to see. We go out of our way to highlight these accomplishments. But then, there are those moments of shame. The parts of our past we'd like to run from and deny as a part of ourselves.

The invitation being offered in Matthew's genealogy is to own all of our past. To cease expending energy trying to deny and keep certain parts of ourselves hidden away. This doesn't mean you have to be proud of it all. You don't have to prominently display those shameful moments. But you do have to own it all. It's a part of you.

The more we are able to embrace our whole selves, the more we allow for the grace and healing of Christ to flow through us.

INVITATION

EMBRACE YOUR WHOLE SELF
BY OWNING ALL THE PARTS OF
YOUR STORY.

SPACE FOR REFLECTION

- Are there any parts of your past you feel uncomfortable owning?

  _____

  _____

  _____

  _____

  _____

  _____

- How does it feel to own those stories as a part of you?

  _____

  _____

  _____

  _____

  _____

  _____

EVERYTHING IS REDEEMABLE

READING: Matthew 1:6

...David was the father of Solomon, whose mother had been Uriah's wife...

Let's take yesterday's reading one step further. It's one thing to embrace your whole story. That's important and necessary. But it's something entirely different to believe that, even with a checkered past, you can still be a person God uses to bring love and grace into the world.

Today, we're going to look a little closer at the phrase "Uriah's wife" because I think there's so much wisdom hidden in these two words.

This is a shameful story. Deceit. Murder. Adultery. Power used to manipulate and take advantage of those without power. At first glance, there's nothing redeeming here. How could anything good come from this?

But, as we saw yesterday, this is one of the stories through which Jesus, the Messiah, was birthed. Good was able to come from a moment even as horrible as this one.

Right away, before we read anything about what Jesus did, we come upon a story rooted in grace. One built upon a foundation of redemption and using our worst moments to birth hope and love into this world.

Here's what I believe: You've made a few mistakes. Had a few stumbles. We've all been there. It's a part of being human.

But here's what I also believe: Those mistakes don't define you. Nor do they mean your story is over. You have a gift to offer the world. Your life is to be a vessel of healing, love, grace, hope, peace, joy, and all the other good, redeeming qualities we need more of.

The story of Christmas begins with a loud declaration: Nothing can stand in the way of God's grace. Everything is redeemable.

This is true for your life as well.

The mistakes. The past sin. Yes, they're there. And they have to be dealt with. Owned and acknowledged.

But they don't disqualify you from being someone God uses to bring healing to this world. You have a role to play in God's restoring work.

Your life matters.

You are valued.

There's nothing that can change that truth.

SPACE FOR REFLECTION

- Have you ever thought yourself unworthy or unqualified because of your past?

  _____

  _____

  _____

  _____

  _____

- How does it feel to hear that God can use your life to bring love and healing to the world?

  _____

  _____

  _____

  _____

  _____

Day
5

"BECAUSE HE WAS A RIGHTEOUS MAN..."

READING: Matthew 1:18–25

This is how the birth of Jesus the Messiah came about: His mother Mary was pledged to be married to Joseph, but before they came together, she was found to be pregnant through the Holy Spirit. Because Joseph her husband was faithful to the law, and yet did not want to expose her to public disgrace, he had in mind to divorce her quietly.

But after he had considered this, an angel of the Lord appeared to him in a dream and said, "Joseph son of David, do not be afraid to take Mary home as your wife, because what is conceived in her is from the Holy Spirit. She will give birth to a son, and you are to give him the name Jesus, because he will save his people from their sins."

All this took place to fulfill what the Lord had said through the prophet: "The virgin will conceive and give birth to a son, and they will call him Immanuel" (which means "God with us").

When Joseph woke up, he did what the angel of the Lord had commanded him and took Mary home as his wife. But he did not consummate their marriage until she gave birth to a son. And he gave him the name Jesus.

Joseph's fiancé is pregnant with a child he knows is not his own. Sounds like the perfect storyline for a daytime talk show. But rather than exposing Mary to public humiliation, Joseph decides to end the engagement and secretly send her away. The reason he does this is "because he was a righteous man."

This is how Matthew introduces us to Mary and Joseph, the parents of Jesus. With a scandal, and with Joseph determined to do the right, religious thing.

At the top of Reece's homework, written in bold, capital letters, was the sentence, "WE FOLLOW THE RULES!" The corresponding assignment was to circle all the people following the rules and describe what rule they were following. It was a helpful assignment for him as he's learning how to interact with others.

Rules are a good thing. They help keep the world operating in an orderly fashion. Without rules, chaos would ensue. But what happens when we elevate rule-following to being the greatest, most sacred pursuit?

When we meet Joseph, he's following the rules. The rules that tell him Mary is not someone to be trusted and he should quietly break the engagement. This is the wisdom he's received from his family, his culture, and his religion.

Then, one night, he has a dream. In this dream, the Spirit visits Joseph and tells him to take Mary as his wife because her pregnancy is the work of the Spirit. Apparently that's all the convincing he needs. No questions asked. No wondering if the dream was legit or just the result of his late-night pizza run. He wakes up, and the engagement is back on.

Why did Joseph need to be asleep for the Spirit to speak? Was it the only time all the other voices in his head were silenced? The voices telling him to play it safe, follow the rules, and do it how everyone in his family and tribe would do it. We all know these voices. They're the background noise we hear every day.

The rules you've been following have brought you to where you are today. But will those same rules allow you to continue growing and expanding as a person? Will they help you become the person the Spirit is leading you to be?

The story of Joseph is an invitation to inspect the rules and wisdom guiding our life. Are they helping you experience the new things that the Spirit is birthing? Are they offering you a greater vision for how you can partner with the Spirit to bring new life and hope to this world? If not, maybe it's time to leave a few rules behind this season and embrace a new wisdom. Sometimes the new can only be birthed when we have the courage to step outside our tradition and beyond the rules we've been living by.

INVITATION

INSPECT THE RULES YOU'VE BEEN
LIVING BY. LEAVE BEHIND ANY
THAT ARE TAKING YOU AWAY FROM
PARTNERING WITH THE SPIRIT TO
BIRTH NEW LIFE AND HOPE WITHIN
YOU AND THE WORLD.

SPACE FOR REFLECTION

- Are you following any rules that have been placed on you by others?

- What rules in your life do you need to let go of today because they aren't leading you deeper into joy?

IMMANUEL

READING: Matthew 1:22–23

All this took place to fulfill what the Lord had said through the prophet: "The virgin will conceive and give birth to a son, and they will call him Immanuel" (which means "God with us").

A friend recently called me. He'd had a fight with one of his kids and wanted to talk about it. By the time we hung up, he was in much better spirits. The heaviness I first heard in his voice was gone and he was hopeful about healing the rift. This is what happens when we share our lives with others.

In Joseph's dream, he's told that the child to be born will be called Immanuel, meaning "God with us." Jesus will be a sign of God's presence with humanity. He will be a symbol of God's eternal faithfulness.

This is the promise with which Matthew begins the story of Jesus, and the promise he concludes with. Here's the final line in his Gospel: "And surely I am with you always, to the very end of the age." (Matthew 28:20) The story begins with the promise of God's presence and ends with the continuing promise of God's presence.

During the years Jesus walked the Earth, that promise would have felt real. There was a physical presence of hope, peace, grace, and love. You could see that presence in human form. You could touch it. Hear it. Today, that promise can feel distant. Our hope in its trustfulness can dwindle.

Yet, Matthew insists that promise continues for us today. And he believes it's you and me who reveal the truth of Immanuel—"God with us." In the final section of his Gospel, Matthew writes what's known as "The Great Commission." It's a command for followers of Jesus to spread the hope of Christ throughout the entire world. He's saying, "As you experience the grace and hope and peace of Christ, you must now bring that same experience to others. It can't stay with you." Matthew is inviting us to embody the presence of God for the world.

Do you know anyone who needs to hear your voice?

Are there any phone calls, texts, or handwritten letters you can send? Can you let someone know they're not alone and someone is thinking about them?

Is there a broken relationship in your life? Can you take the first step today in healing what's been lost?

Or, maybe the promise of God's presence is a hope you need to discover this season. May you find the courage to share your life, and as you do, may you experience the hope and peace of Christ.

INVITATION

BE THE PRESENCE OF GOD FOR
THIS WORLD, BRINGING HOPE,
PEACE, GRACE, AND LOVE TO OTHERS
THROUGH YOUR LIFE.

SPACE FOR REFLECTION

- Who needs the gift of your presence today?

Day 7

THE GIFT OF SILENCE

READING:
Luke 1:5–22, 67–79

In the time of Herod king of Judea there was a priest named Zechariah, who belonged to the priestly division of Abijah; his wife Elizabeth was also a descendant of Aaron. Both of them were righteous in the sight of God, observing all the Lord's commands and decrees blamelessly. But they were childless because Elizabeth was not able to conceive, and they were both very old.

Once when Zechariah's division was on duty and he was serving as priest before God, he was chosen by lot, according to the custom of the priesthood, to go into the temple of the Lord and burn incense. And when the time for the burning of incense came, all the assembled worshipers were praying outside.

Then an angel of the Lord appeared to him, standing at the right side of the altar of incense. When

Zechariah saw him, he was startled and was gripped with fear. But the angel said to him: "Do not be afraid, Zechariah; your prayer has been heard. Your wife Elizabeth will bear you a son, and you are to call him John. He will be a joy and delight to you, and many will rejoice because of his birth, for he will be great in the sight of the Lord. He is never to take wine or other fermented drink, and he will be filled with the Holy Spirit even before he is born. He will bring back many of the people of Israel to the Lord their God. And he will go on before the Lord, in the spirit and power of Elijah, to turn the hearts of the parents to their children and the disobedient to the wisdom of the righteous—to make ready a people prepared for the Lord."

Zechariah asked the angel, "How can I be sure of this? I am an old man and my wife is well along in years."

The angel said to him, "I am Gabriel. I stand in the presence of God, and I have been sent to speak to you and to tell you this good news. And now you will be silent and not able to speak until the day this happens, because you did not believe my words, which will come true at their appointed time."

Meanwhile, the people were waiting for Zechariah and wondering why he stayed so long in the temple. When he came out, he could not speak to them. They realized he had seen a vision in the temple, for he kept making signs to them but remained unable to speak.

His father Zechariah was filled with the Holy Spirit and prophesied:

"Praise be to the Lord, the God of Israel,
    because he has come to his people and redeemed them.
He has raised up a horn of salvation for us
    in the house of his servant David
(as he said through his holy prophets of long ago),
salvation from our enemies
    and from the hand of all who hate us—
to show mercy to our ancestors
    and to remember his holy covenant,
the oath he swore to our father Abraham:
to rescue us from the hand of our enemies,
    and to enable us to serve him without fear
in holiness and righteousness before him all our days.

And you, my child, will be called a prophet of the Most High;
    for you will go on before the Lord to prepare the way for him,
to give his people the knowledge of salvation
    through the forgiveness of their sins,
because of the tender mercy of our God,
    by which the rising sun will come to us from heaven
to shine on those living in darkness
    and in the shadow of death,
to guide our feet into the path of peace."

How much of your life is spent communicating? How much time do you spend talking, posting online, writing emails, and sending texts?

Now, imagine the ability to communicate was taken away from you for a season. How would you respond? How might that experience change you?

This is how we are introduced to Zechariah. I know that's not a name that often comes to mind when thinking about the story of Christmas. He gets no love from Christmas pageants, but he has a pivotal role to play in what Luke has to say about Jesus. To Luke, the story of Zechariah acts as a prelude to the birth of Jesus. He's the opening act responsible for firing up the crowd.

One day, while at work, Zechariah is visited by an angel who tells Zechariah that his wife, Elizabeth, will give birth to a son whom they are to name John. His response is one of disbelief. Surely he and Elizabeth are too old! The angel finds his lack of faith disturbing and immediately silences Zechariah until the day his son will be born. "And now you will be silent and not able to speak until the day this happens..." (Luke 1:20)

In a world before the internet and smartphones, Zechariah has essentially lost all ability to communicate. He has been forced into a season of silence.

Luke returns to Zechariah's story a few months later. His son is born and he can now speak again. We are given a glimpse into how a season of silence has changed Zechariah. He returns to the world of speech with a song. A song of thanksgiving. There's no bitterness. No anger at the Spirit for taking away his ability to communicate. There's only joy and a deep hope for what's about to take place through Jesus.

All this would not have been possible had it not been for the silence. The forced silence that first appeared as a punishment is now seen as a gift. An opportunity for Zechariah to shut up and listen.

Silence changes us. It helps us discover what we are carrying within. It helps us listen to the Spirit of hope that we silence with the noise we produce. For Zechariah, he had given up hope that he and his wife would ever have a child. It was the silence that rebirthed hope within him.

"Silence is the mystery of the world to come. Speech is the organ of this present world. More than all things love silence: it brings you a fruit that the tongue cannot describe. In the beginning we have to force ourselves to be silent. But then from our very silence is born something that draws us into deeper silence. May God give you an experience of this 'something' that is born of silence. If you practice this, inexpressible light will dawn upon you."

—Isaac of Nineveh (seventh-century Syrian bishop)

INVITATION

CREATE SPACE IN YOUR LIFE FOR
SILENCE. FIND A TIME TO SET ASIDE ALL
FORMS OF COMMUNICATION
AND LISTEN. MAYBE YOU'D LIKE TO
JOURNAL WHAT YOU HEAR.

SPACE FOR REFLECTION

- As you carve out time to be silent and listen, what do you hear?

Day 8

STEPPING INTO THE DISRUPTION

READING: Luke 1:26–38

In the sixth month of Elizabeth's pregnancy, God sent the angel Gabriel to Nazareth, a town in Galilee, to a virgin pledged to be married to a man named Joseph, a descendant of David. The virgin's name was Mary. The angel went to her and said, "Greetings, you who are highly favored! The Lord is with you."

Mary was greatly troubled at his words and wondered what kind of greeting this might be. But the angel said to her, "Do not be afraid, Mary; you have found favor with God. You will conceive and give birth to a son, and you are to call him Jesus. He will be great and will be called the Son of the Most High. The Lord God will give him the throne of his father David, and he will reign over Jacob's descendants forever; his kingdom will never end."

"How will this be," Mary asked the angel, "since I am a virgin?"

The angel answered, "The Holy Spirit will come on you, and the power of the Most High will overshadow you. So the holy one to be born will be called the Son of God. Even Elizabeth your relative is going to have a child in her old age, and she who was said to be unable to conceive is in her sixth month. For no word from God will ever fail."

"I am the Lord's servant," Mary answered. "May your word to me be fulfilled." Then the angel left her.

Let's return to the story of Mary.

A few years ago, I took an unexpected two months off work. I was experiencing mysterious health symptoms that a doctor told me were most likely stress related. For weeks, I'd been fighting how I was feeling. I'd sit at my desk trying to work on sermons, but there was nothing there. Within me there was no life. The joy I once felt for my work was gone.

I would have carried on like this indefinitely had it not been for the advice of my doctor who told me I needed to take some time off. All the signs had been pointing in this direction for a while. I was too stubborn to listen. The more I dug my heels in and resisted, the more my health suffered. And the more anxious I became as I felt the joy being drained from me.

I consider this season in my life a major time of disruption. It wasn't a disruption I was ready for and one I wasn't eager to embrace.

Disruption is at the heart of the Christmas story. Yes, there's joy and hope and all the good things we associate with the birth of Jesus. But what about the fear? The confusion? The uncertainty? The necessity of leaving behind that which is safe, comfortable, and familiar in order to embrace the new?

Notice how Mary responds when the angel Gabriel first visits her:

> *"Mary was greatly troubled at his words and wondered what kind of greeting this might be." (Luke 1:29)*

This is how we're introduced to Mary in Luke's Gospel. She's greatly troubled. The Greek word used for trouble in this passage conveys an inner state in great turmoil from heightened emotions. We've all been there, our stomachs churning and anxious thoughts running through our minds. Mary doesn't know whether to cut and run or sit and listen.

By the end of her conversation with Gabriel, she appears to be on board with the plan and simply responds with, "I am the Lord's servant. May it be to me as you have said."

Mary has said yes to the disruption. Which raises the question, could she have said no? Maybe Mary wasn't the first woman invited by the Spirit to participate in the birthing of Christ into the world. But it's Mary who says yes to stepping into the disruption.

The birthing of all new things begins with a willingness to step into the disruptions life brings our way. Yes, it will cost us. We will be forced to relearn. Forced to let go of what we find familiar or comfortable. But fighting or resisting the disruptions in front of us will only take us away from the life and joy we truly desire. And who knows what waits on the other side? It could be the beginning of a new journey beyond what you thought possible.

More to come…

INVITATION

STEP INTO THE DISRUPTIONS YOU FIND YOURSELF FACING, TRUSTING THIS IS AN INVITATION FROM THE SPIRIT TO BIRTH SOMETHING NEW WITHIN YOU.

SPACE FOR REFLECTION

- What are the disruptions you currently find yourself facing in life?

- What would it look like for you to step into and embrace those disruptions?

THE HILL COUNTRY

READING: Luke 1:39–40

At that time Mary got ready and hurried to a town in the hill country of Judea, where she entered Zechariah's home and greeted Elizabeth.

Once the angel leaves Mary, she immediately heads to the "hill country" for a three-month stay at the home of Zechariah and Elizabeth whom we met the other day. Mary is retreating to a place of solitude. She needs space to reflect on the disruption she's stepping into and prepare for what's to come.

All disruptions bring change. This is true for both welcome and unwelcome disruptions. A disruption signals an end to what was. A new future is opening before us. Time in the hill country is necessary for helping make sense of what that change will look like.

Luke doesn't tell us exactly what happened during Mary's time of retreat, but we can speculate.

First, Mary needed time alone. She needed to be away from all that was familiar and all that could distract her. Chances are she didn't leave a forwarding address for anyone to track her down. There was probably no Wi-Fi signal in the hill country which meant she didn't spend her days watching YouTube clips or scrolling through Instagram reels. I'd guess she spent a lot of time in silence. Walking through the hills. Praying. Journaling her innermost thoughts.

Second, Mary was seeking mentors. The angel told Mary that Elizabeth, her relative, was also having a baby. So we know Elizabeth was an older woman who was six months ahead of Mary in the miraculous baby department. Was Elizabeth someone Mary often looked to for wisdom? Was she a trusted mentor in Mary's life? Mary needed the support and wisdom of someone who was a bit further down the road than her. Elizabeth was that guide.

Third, Mary had to grieve what she was leaving behind. You can't fully embrace the new until you acknowledge what is being lost. Mary's dreams of a normal life were gone when the angel told her she'd be giving birth to

Jesus, the Son of God. That's bound to change your life a bit! Mary had to make space within herself for receiving this new future by being honest with all she was leaving behind in the process.

INVITATION

SPEND TIME IN RETREAT:
REFLECT AND JOURNAL THE THOUGHTS
YOU'RE CARRYING WITHIN YOURSELF.
FIND MENTORS WHO CAN GUIDE
YOU THROUGH THE SPACE YOU'RE IN.
GRIEVE WHAT IS BEING LEFT BEHIND AS
YOU WALK FORWARD INTO THE NEW.

Space for Reflection

- As you spend intentional time in solitude, do any new or surprising thoughts come to mind? Is there any new awareness of your inner life?

  _____

  _____

  _____

- Who are your mentors? (The people you look to for wisdom and advice.)

  _____

  _____

  _____

- Are there any losses in your life you have not properly grieved? The loss of an unfulfilled dream needs to be grieved as much as the loss of a loved one.

  _____

  _____

  _____

  _____

Day 10

STAY HUNGRY

READING: Luke 1:46–55

And Mary said:

"My soul glorifies the Lord
*   and my spirit rejoices in God my Savior,*
for he has been mindful
*   of the humble state of his servant.*
From now on all generations will call me blessed,
*   for the Mighty One has done great things for me—*
*   holy is his name.*
His mercy extends to those who fear him,
*   from generation to generation.*
He has performed mighty deeds with his arm;
*   he has scattered those who are proud in their inmost*
thoughts.
He has brought down rulers from their thrones
*   but has lifted up the humble.*

He has filled the hungry with good things
but has sent the rich away empty.
He has helped his servant Israel,
remembering to be merciful
to Abraham and his descendants forever,
just as he promised our ancestors."

Today's Scripture comes from Mary's time in the hill country. These verses are the only words we get from Mary during those three months of hibernation. They take the form of a song.

One of the ideas found within these lines is the danger of having too much. Mary has realized the "good things" of God come to those whose lives aren't crammed full of stuff. People who still have space left within themselves to receive.

So, what are these good things? I'd suggest they're the gifts of Advent: hope, love, joy, and peace. These are gifts the Spirit births deep within. They can't be bought. You can't acquire them by consuming more.

When Reece was younger, we'd often pick out a new Hot Wheels car on our Target runs. It's how I got him to sit in the shopping cart. He'd play with it for a few days, then by the next trip, he was ready for another car. If I didn't let him get a car, we'd have trouble. As a three-year-old, his joy was based on possessing a new car. This is a fleeting joy. It's a shallow peace that's swayed by external situations. The good things of God are found deeper. It's a hope not determined by how much you own, or how well you're doing compared to everyone else. It's love with a foundation that's deeper than feelings that come and go.

For the first time in human history, we live in a world where more people are dying from eating too much rather than from too little.

Our excess is literally killing us. It's destroying us from the inside.

And it seems the more we have, the more we want.

According to studies, the average size of the American home has tripled in the past fifty years.[1]

Most household moves outside the US weigh 2,500 to 7,500 pounds. Within the US, the average household move weighs 8,500 pounds, the weight of a full-grown hippo![2]

---

1   Joshua Becker, 21 Surprising Statistics That Reveal How Much Stuff We Actually Own, https://www.becomingminimalist.com/clutter-stats/ (accessed August 13, 2023)

2   Josh Sanburn, America's Clutter Problem, TIME Magazine, March 12, 2015, https://time.com/3741849/americas-clutter-problem/ (accessed August 13, 2023)

To contain this hippo we're dragging behind us, we need more space—thus, the rise of storage facilities.

The US has more than 50,000 storage facilities, more than five times the number of Starbucks across the country! This equates to 7.3 square feet of storage space for everyone in the country. Storage facilities are in such abundance, everyone in the US could simultaneously fit inside one.[3]

What if our pursuit of more, of thinking we can acquire the good life through material pursuit, is squeezing out the good things God desires to gift our lives with?

What if the hope, love, peace, and joy we truly desire is found in our hunger? What if it's found as we ask the Spirit to birth these ways of life within us instead of trying to fill that empty space with that which we can acquire on our own?

INVITATION

TAKE THE TIME TO ASK IF THERE'S ANYTHING IN YOUR LIFE SQUEEZING OUT THE "GOOD THINGS" OF GOD.

---

3   Ibid.

SPACE FOR REFLECTION

- Have you ever considered hunger as something positive?

  ....
  ....
  ....
  ....
  ....
  ....

- How do you think abundance can cause us to miss out on hope, love, peace, and joy?

  ....
  ....
  ....
  ....
  ....
  ....

THERE
AND BACK
AGAIN

READING: Luke 1:56

Mary stayed with Elizabeth for about three months and then returned home.

When Bilbo is returning home from his adventure with Gandalf in *The Hobbit*, he comes to the Elvish town of Rivendell. Here's how Tolkien describes their return:

"It was on May the First that the two came back at last to the brink of the valley of Rivendell, where stood the Last (or the First) Homely House."[4]

---

4   J.R.R. Tolkien (1982). *The Hobbit*. Ballantine Books

Do you see the wisdom here?

The Homely House that Bilbo sees is either the first or the last house on the journey. It's a matter of perspective. On his way out of town, it's the last house. On his return, it's the first.

That's what happens. We experience a disruption, spend some time in the hill country trying to understand what the change will mean for us, and then we return home with our newfound wisdom. It's the classic storyline played out in movies and books. It's what author Joseph Campbell has termed "The Hero's Journey." The main character faces a crisis, discovers how to overcome that crisis, and returns home. But their experience has changed them. The last house has now become the first house. They see the world differently.

After Mary spends three months in the hill country, Luke tells us she returns home. This verse isn't a throwaway line. It's telling us Mary has changed. She's continuing to accept her role in birthing Jesus into the world and is now ready to offer this gift to her community.

Mary didn't have to return home. She could have left for another village. Another country. Regardless of what excuse she or Joseph offered for her pregnancy, there would have been odd looks coming her way. Who's really going to believe an unwed, pregnant teenager saying they're carrying the Holy Spirit's child? Would she have lost friends? Would her family have scorned her?

Mary knows she's in for a rough time, but she returns home anyway. Her time in solitude with Elizabeth has prepared her. She's been strengthened by the Spirit. And she's returning with wisdom she didn't possess earlier. A deeper understanding of what this child will mean for her people and the world. She understands that she can't withhold this gift.

The disruptions we face in life will change us. There's no stopping that. What we can control is how we'll respond to the disruption. Will we allow bitterness to creep into our soul? Upset at the turns life has taken? Or, will we walk through the disruptions with openness? And, like Mary, return home with a gift birthed by the Spirit in the chaos of disruption.

INVITATION

SEE THE DISRUPTIONS IN YOUR LIFE AS AN OPPORTUNITY FOR GROWTH.

SPACE FOR REFLECTION

- Have any disruptions in your life led to a bitterness within your heart?

- What wisdom have you gained from the disruptions you've faced in life?

- How can you offer to your community the gifts of what you've learned?

Day
12

FREEDOM!

Luke 1:67–75

His father Zechariah was filled with the Holy
Spirit and prophesied:

"Praise be to the Lord, the God of Israel,
  because he has come to his people and redeemed them.
He has raised up a horn of salvation for us
  in the house of his servant David
(as he said through his holy prophets of long ago),
salvation from our enemies
  and from the hand of all who hate us—
to show mercy to our ancestors
  and to remember his holy covenant,
  the oath he swore to our father Abraham:
to rescue us from the hand of our enemies,
  and to enable us to serve him without fear
  in holiness and righteousness before him all our
days..."

"Aye, fight and you may die. Run, and you'll live... at least a while. And dying in your beds, many years from now, would you be willin' to trade ALL the days, from this day to that, for one chance, just one chance, to come back here and tell our enemies that they may take our lives, but they'll never take... OUR FREEDOM!"[5]

This scene from *Braveheart* gets your blood pumping! It's that pivotal moment when William Wallace, played by Mel Gibson, with face painted blue, rallies the Scots to fight against the English army for their freedom.

We're all after a life of freedom. For William Wallace and the Scots, it was freedom from the English. Freedom to be their own rulers. For us, maybe that type of freedom isn't on our radar. But we still desire freedom in our own way. Freedom from addiction. Freedom from self-defeating thoughts or behaviors. Freedom from others and any unhealthy expectations they place on us. Within all of us is this longing to be free. To embody the truest expression of the person we've been created to be.

When Zechariah (see Day 8) bursts into song following his time of silence, this is exactly the sentiment he

---

5   Mel Gibson (1995). *Braveheart*. Paramount Pictures

expresses: "to rescue us from the hand of our enemies, and to enable us to serve him without fear." (Luke 1:74)

This line brings us back to an earlier time in Jewish history, that of the Exodus. When Moses is famously telling Pharaoh to "Let my people go!" the reason he gives is so they can worship God in freedom. (Exodus 4:23 and 9:1)

God has always sought freedom for us. Freedom from oppressive rulers, yes. But also freedom from all that enslaves us in life. When this line rolls off Zechariah's lips, he's expressing his hope that Jesus will be this Savior. That Jesus will usher in a new exodus when God will save and rescue his people from all that holds us in bondage.

Now, this freedom comes with a specific purpose. Moses and Zechariah both proclaim that the purpose of this freedom is so we can serve/worship God. While worship is often understood as the songs we sing in a church service, Moses and Zechariah are expressing something more expansive. They're talking about the way we live the entirety of our lives. How we love our neighbor. How we love ourselves. What we pursue with our time and money. To Zechariah and Moses, we worship God by expressing love in the world. Every moment is an opportunity to worship.

Zechariah's song expresses this universal desire we have within to be set free from the sin and brokenness preventing us from receiving and expressing love. He's envisioning a world where our pain is healed. A world that doesn't run on greed and self-serving pursuits, but a world that's founded on love. His hope is that Jesus will be the one to lead us into this freedom.

You were made to love. This is who you are as your truest, deepest self.

Christ comes to show us that the path of love is the path of freedom. His birth announces this great love upon each of us, and we are now being invited to offer that love to others through our lives.

This season, let's look for the opportunities to show love to others. Living in this way is how we embody the truest and most free version of ourselves.

INVITATION

WORSHIP GOD THIS SEASON BY FOLLOWING JESUS DOWN THE PATH OF LOVE.

SPACE FOR REFLECTION

- Have you ever felt more alive through an act of love?

  _____

  _____

  _____

  _____

- Where can you worship God this season through acts of love?

  _____

  _____

  _____

  _____

- Who can you show love to?

  _____

  _____

  _____

  _____

CAESAR AUGUSTUS

READING: Luke 2:1–14

In those days Caesar Augustus issued a decree that a census should be taken of the entire Roman world. (This was the first census that took place while Quirinius was governor of Syria.) And everyone went to their own town to register.

So Joseph also went up from the town of Nazareth in Galilee to Judea, to Bethlehem the town of David, because he belonged to the house and line of David. He went there to register with Mary, who was pledged to be married to him and was expecting a child. While they were there, the time came for the baby to be born, and she gave birth to her firstborn, a son. She wrapped him in cloths and placed him in a manger, because there was no guest room available for them.

And there were shepherds living out in the fields nearby, keeping watch over their flocks at night. An angel of the Lord appeared to them, and the glory of the Lord shone around them, and they were terrified. But the angel said to them, "Do not be afraid. I bring you good news that will cause great joy for all the people. Today in the town of David a Savior has been born to you; he is the Messiah, the Lord. This will be a sign to you: You will find a baby wrapped in cloths and lying in a manger."

Suddenly a great company of the heavenly host appeared with the angel, praising God and saying,

"Glory to God in the highest heaven,
*   and on earth peace to those on whom his favor rests."*

Before we arrive at the birth of Jesus, we're introduced to Caesar Augustus, an important figure for understanding the story of Christmas.

Here's how Caesar Augustus became Caesar Augustus, the first emperor of Rome.

First, Caesar.

At birth, Augustus was named Gaius Octavius. When he became the adopted son of Julius Caesar, he took the name Gaius Julius Caesar, but was more widely known as Octavian. In 44 BCE, his adoptive father, Julius Caesar, was assassinated. When the Senate ruled in favor of posthumously granting Julius Caesar divine status, our boy Octavian became known as "son of the divine Julius" or "son of the god." All this would have been swirling in the air when Luke mentions Caesar in his Gospel.

Second, Augustus.

The Roman Republic was constantly embroiled in civil war until the Battle of Actium in 31 BCE. At this time, Octavian defeated his enemies, leaving him sole ruler of the Roman world. On his return to Rome, he officially took the title Augustus, meaning "Revered One," and established himself as the first emperor of the entire Roman empire. Caesar Augustus was born.

All throughout the empire, a message of good news was proclaimed heralding Caesar Augustus as "Savior of the world." The one who had brought peace to earth by ending all civil wars and ushering in the Pax Romana (Roman peace).

If you were alive in the world at this time, you knew who ruled the world. You knew who brought salvation and peace to the world. You knew who the son of God was. His image was everywhere you looked. Here's Caesar

Augustus, the one who calms the chaos, bringing order and the dawning of a new day! He is the one we are to follow and pledge our allegiance to. His rule is to be a source of joy and hope for all.

Then Luke goes and ruins the narrative.

The very things proclaimed and spoken about Augustus are now being placed on this child, Jesus.

Clearly, Luke and others long for a different ruler on the throne. The claims made about Augustus and what his rule accomplished must not have proven true for everyone. Otherwise, there would have been no need for another Savior of the world. For those who weren't experiencing the salvation, peace, and joy of Augustus's rule, the advent of a new Savior would have sparked hope. It would have been a welcome announcement of good news, loudly proclaiming:

"There is another coming who will lead you into the peace and joy your heart desires."

INVITATION

REFLECT ON ALL THAT PROMISES SALVATION, PEACE, HOPE, AND JOY.

SPACE FOR REFLECTION

- Who or what in our world promises salvation, peace, hope, and joy?

- Have you been placing your hopes in those promises?

- Do you find those promises being fulfilled in your life?

Day 14

PEACE ON EARTH

READING: Luke 2:8–14

And there were shepherds living out in the fields nearby, keeping watch over their flocks at night. An angel of the Lord appeared to them, and the glory of the Lord shone around them, and they were terrified. But the angel said to them, "Do not be afraid. I bring you good news that will cause great joy for all the people. Today in the town of David a Savior has been born to you; he is the Messiah, the Lord. This will be a sign to you: You will find a baby wrapped in cloths and lying in a manger."

Suddenly a great company of the heavenly host appeared with the angel, praising God and saying,

"Glory to God in the highest heaven,
*   and on earth peace to those on whom his favor*
*   rests."*

I'm a big fan of the Jack Reacher series. It's my go-to when I need a light read.

The plot of every book follows the same basic pattern. There are some bad guys who do some bad things. Jack Reacher happens to stumble upon these bad guys and swoops in to save the day, reestablishing peace and order. For Reacher, the way to peace is through his fists and firepower. You know the storyline. It shows up again and again. Victory is achieved through violence.

Augustus's reign ushered in the Pax Romana (Roman peace). All warring factions had been defeated, leaving Augustus free to rule over the entire Roman empire. It was to be a time of rejoicing. War was no more. The only problem was the path of violence Augustus and the Roman empire took to secure and maintain that peace. It was a path that worked for some, but not for all.

Like any James Bond villain, Rome sought global domination. They wanted their empire to extend to the ends of the earth and were constantly bringing other tribes under their rule. Their sales pitch: "Join us and experience the peace of Rome." Not everyone willingly signed up. But Rome didn't care; they'd conquer them anyway by killing all those who stood in their way of global domination. As one opposing leader described Rome's endless drive for more territory: "They make a desert and call it peace." Rome was claiming to be bringing salvation to foreign lands, but in reality they brought massive destruction and upheaval. This wasn't true peace on earth.

And then there were the taxes required to maintain the empire. Why did Mary and Joseph travel to Bethlehem to register for Augustus's census? Because empires need to boast about how large they are and make sure everyone is paying their dues to keep the military machine going. Ancient records show the financial burden imposed by Roman taxes was so large, multitudes found themselves needing to leave their land so they could look for work elsewhere. This created a massive refugee crisis.

Roman peace was established and maintained by the sword. The authorities ruled with violence and oppression, killing anyone opposed to their way of life.

Jesus was born during Pax Romana, bringing that same promise of peace. Yet, this is a peace that comes through a different means. This is a peace that's established through love and sacrifice. It's a peace rooted in grace and forgiveness and mercy. The peace of Jesus stands in direct contrast to the peace of Rome.

Advent is an invitation to inspect which path to peace we are placing our trust in. What do we believe is the best way to bring peace and healing to our world? Is it the path of Jack Reacher and Rome, with fists and superior firepower? Or, like Jesus, do we trust that true, lasting peace will only come through mercy, forgiveness, love, and sacrifice?

INSPECT WHETHER THE PATH
YOU'RE FOLLOWING IS LEADING
YOU TO TRUE PEACE.

SPACE FOR REFLECTION

- What do you believe is the path to true peace? Violence? Or sacrifice, forgiveness, and love?

- Which path does our world tend to favor?

- Which path do you find yourself following?

GOOD NEWS OF GREAT JOY

READING: Luke 2:10

"I bring you good news of great joy that will be for all the people."

Good news that will bring great joy?

Sign me up! That's the kind of news I want to wake up to every morning! Would anyone ever say no to a little more joy in their life?

When Luke writes about the joy this good news is to produce, he uses the Greek word "chara." By using this word, he's speaking about a particular type of joy. A joy that originates from the grace of Christ.

Sometimes, the joy we desperately desire is lacking because of the messages we have chosen to place our trust in. The angel's message to the shepherds is an invitation to trust that they are enough. It is a pronouncement of the favor, love, and joy of God that rests upon them. This grace is true regardless of how they feel about themselves. The only question is whether the shepherds will choose to believe it.

The other day, Kitt wasn't listening and I got mad at her. She became upset and ran into her room, crying. A few minutes later, I went to console her. I gave her a big hug and told her I loved her.

When she finally started calming down, she looked at me and asked, "Do you love me even when I do bad things?"

She wanted to know if I loved her all the time, or only when she was behaving. Was my love conditional, or did it waver depending on how I was feeling?

Now, this chain of events wasn't an isolated occurence. This is pretty much how it goes every time we have to correct her behavior. Despite telling her how much we love her no matter how she's behaving, she still questions that love. She still wants to hear that our love for her doesn't change.

Like the announcement of God's favor proclaimed over the shepherds, our love isn't dependent on Kitt's merit or performance. It's an unconditional love rooted in grace.

Just like Kitt wanted reassurance about our love for her, Advent comes to assure us that we are loved just as we are. It's an annual reminder that the angel's message of joy, rooted in grace, isn't just for the shepherds; it's a truth for all of us.

The favor, love, and joy of God is over your life. The invitation of Advent is to trust that message. It's to trust that you are loved, no matter what your year has looked like. You are enough, regardless of how you may be feeling about yourself in this moment.

What you choose to believe about yourself directly affects your experience with joy.

How much joy is stolen from our lives seeking the love we already possess?

How much energy is spent in our attempt to prove or earn the worth and value that has already been announced over us?

This Advent season, will you trust that the favor and joy of God is upon your life?

Will you trust the angel's message of your immeasurable worth and value?

Will you trust that you are enough?

TRUST THE GRACE THAT'S BEEN SPOKEN OVER YOUR LIFE.

SPACE FOR REFLECTION

- Do you ever find yourself trying to prove your worth to God, others, or yourself?

  _____

  _____

  _____

  _____

- What do you think when you hear that you are loved just as you are?

  _____

  _____

  _____

  _____

Day
16

YOUR
EARNEST
DESIRES

READING: Luke 2:15–16

When the angels had left them and gone into heaven, the shepherds said to one another, "Let's go to Bethlehem and see this thing that has happened, which the Lord has told us about."

So they hurried off and found Mary and Joseph, and the baby, who was lying in the manger.

One night, there were shepherds in a field pulling the midnight shift. They were going about their business when an angel appeared in the sky with a message of good news. A child had been born. This child was to be a source of joy and peace.

Upon hearing this message, Luke tells us the shepherds hurried off to see if what they heard was true.

The phrase "hurried off" comes from the Greek word "speudó." It conveys urgency because of an earnest desire. Not just desire. Earnest desire. This is taking desire and cranking the dial beyond ten.

When I was dating Steph, I took a two-week trip to the Czech Republic. This was early in our relationship, and I couldn't wait to get home to see her. After the plane landed at JFK, I made it to my apartment in Westchester, dropped my bags, and immediately hurried off to New York City where she was living. I didn't care about the jet lag or anything else that had piled up from two weeks away. I had an earnest desire to spend time with her and dropped all else to make it happen.

This is how Luke describes the shepherds' response to the angel's announcement of good news. There was a sense of urgency birthed from an earnest desire.

What could these shepherds have so earnestly desired that they immediately hurried off to Bethlehem?

The same things you earnestly desire.

Love. Acceptance. Joy. Inner peace. Connection with others. Forgiveness. A deeply fulfilling, meaningful life. Broken relationships to be mended. To feel whole.

These are the desires at the heart of our shared human experience. They're longings we carry deep within us.

We're not told if any shepherds stayed behind that night. But it wouldn't surprise me if at least one did. The shepherds are human like us. They've had their share of heartbreak. They've experienced disappointment with what they've placed their faith in: God, others, themselves, and the organizations they've been involved with. They've stepped out, taken risks, hoping to see the fulfillment of their desires, but plans didn't go as expected. Like you and me, they have every reason to bury their hearts and protect themselves from ever stepping out and being disappointed again.

But we're told the shepherds hurried off. They chose hope over cynicism.

Is there any good news worth believing in?

Is God still present and at work in this world?

Is there any hope and goodness left in the universe?

These are the questions the shepherds asked before hurrying off to the manger. They're the same questions this story raises for us today.

Advent is an invitation to take a risk again. To believe there is still good news worth putting your trust in. Good news that will lead you into that which your heart earnestly desires.

Like the shepherds, may you find the courage this season to choose hope over cynicism and to believe there are still things in this world that can deliver what they promise.

INVITATION

CHOOSE HOPE OVER CYNICISM.

SPACE FOR REFLECTION

- Why can it be easier to fall into cynicism instead of choosing hope?

  _____

  _____

  _____

  _____

- Are there any cynical thoughts you can leave behind this Advent season?

  _____

  _____

  _____

  _____

  _____

JOYLESS URGENCY

READING: Luke 2:15–18

When the angels had left them and gone into heaven, the shepherds said to one another, "Let's go to Bethlehem and see this thing that has happened, which the Lord has told us about."

So they hurried off and found Mary and Joseph, and the baby, who was lying in the manger. When they had seen him, they spread the word concerning what had been told them about this child, and all who heard it were amazed at what the shepherds said to them.

It was sometime around 5:30 when Reece woke me up and asked, "Are we ready to decorate the Christmas tree now?" Anytime he knows something special is happening, he's ready to go long before anyone else in the house. It's the reason we don't tell him when Christmas is. I don't think he'd sleep the night before.

I wish I could say this is a rare occurrence, but it doesn't take much to get him excited and ready to go that early in the morning. Every day is a new adventure filled with new discoveries to be made. He holds an expectation for what's to come.

Expectation is what the shepherds traveled to Bethlehem with. The angel promised that joy would be found at the manger and that's what they expected to find there. That expectation produced wonder, awe, and excitement. This is everything I see on display in Reece as he waits excitedly to decorate the tree.

For the shepherds, the joy and wonder didn't stop when they laid their eyes on Jesus. Luke tells us they went and spread the message of what they had found and "all who heard it were amazed at what the shepherds said to them." Their joy couldn't be contained. It flowed from their being and spread to those around them. It was contagious.

For both my kids, joy comes naturally. They don't have to do much to capture it. A sheet of stickers from the checkout line or an empty cardboard box, and they're good to go.

As we get older, it seems we have to be more intentional about living from a place of joy. The author Marilynne Robinson has described the "spirit of our times as one of joyless urgency." I recognize this spirit in myself far too often. It's that anxious, rushed feeling you have when you're trying to get everything done as quickly as possible, so you can check it off your list and get to the next task.

In such a system, life becomes an endless slog, leaving you burdened and overwhelmed with no room for joy. There's no expectation that something new and wondrous might be waiting around the corner. You're just trying to make it through the day so you can repeat it all over again tomorrow. And, just like the amazement that spread out from the shepherds, this joyless urgency is contagious as well. You can feel it in the air.

So, how do we combat the spirit of joyless urgency we often find ourselves being pulled toward?

How do we live with expectation about the joy to come, rather than believing our best moments of joy lie in the past?

We live each day in radical amazement.

The Jewish author Abraham Joshua Heschel made his daily prayer one of asking God for wonder rather than success or wisdom. Heschel found the wonder he desired and offered guidance for how to capture it:

"Our goal should be to live life in radical amazement... get up in the morning and look at the world in a way that takes nothing for granted. Everything is phenomenal; everything is incredible; never treat life casually."

Each year, Advent comes rushing in with an invitation to recapture joy by living in radical amazement. There's beauty and wonder hidden in every moment. Will we open our eyes to that beauty or pass right by as we joylessly hurry from one moment to the next?

INVITATION

LIVE EACH DAY WITH RADICAL AMAZEMENT.

Space for Reflection

- Do you ever experience this "joyless urgency" Marilynne Robinson writes about?

_____

_____

_____

_____

_____

- What does it look like to live each day in radical amazement?

_____

_____

_____

_____

_____

Day
18

RETURNING HOME WITH PRAISE

READING: Luke 2:20

The shepherds returned, glorifying and praising God for all the things they had heard and seen, which were just as they had been told.

When you return home from a trip as eventful as that of the shepherds, emotions are high and there's a sense of excitement. You can't wait to share with everyone what you've experienced. You have pictures to show and stories to tell. Naïvely, you might even believe the feeling of euphoria in your heart will continue indefinitely. How could it not after the trip you've had!

This is where the shepherds are at this moment. The original intent of their journey, finding a child who will bring great hope and joy, had been fulfilled. God had been faithful to them, and their hearts were filled with praise. I'm sure they were continuing to tell their stories to everyone who would listen.

But what happens when that feeling of joy begins to fade? What happens when you return home to all the worries and anxieties that were present before you left? The unread mail. Bills to be paid. Phone calls to be returned. Doctor's visits. Aging parents. School. Work.

How do we keep that full heart of praise and thankfulness when we wake up and find things right back where they were before?

Gratitude.

It's what the shepherds were expressing on their way home. And it's what would have continued to keep them going when their initial joy began to dim.

Years back, I came upon a study showing how our brains are hardwired to focus on the negative. If you get ten emails in a day – nine praising you and one saying how rotten you are – you will spend the rest of the day (and night) focusing on that one negative email. It's been said the negative sticks to our brains like Velcro, but the positive falls away like Teflon.

This tells me two things. One, we need to be intentional about rewiring our default. And two, this rewiring must be continual. You have to keep at it.

For me, having a gratitude practice has been tremendously helpful in this pursuit. It goes like this: find a set time when you can record, in a journal, the top five things you are grateful for that day. This usually works best before going to bed after you've experienced a full day, and it allows your brain to focus on gratitude as you drift off to sleep.

What this does, like our hope sightings from Day 2, is train our brains to look for things to be grateful for. The longer you practice this, the more you'll find yourself looking around for reasons to be grateful in each moment. Or, when you do hit that rut in the road, you'll be able to refocus your attention on gratitude rather than spinning your wheels and carving out a deeper rut.

There's plenty to complain about. You know this. And we all know people whose attention is focused here. But that way of living will never produce the joy you desire for your life. Like the shepherds returning home with songs of praise and thankfulness, let's fill our hearts with gratitude and continue growing more joy in our hearts each day.

INVITATION

KEEP A GRATITUDE JOURNAL.

SPACE FOR REFLECTION

- Use the next few pages to record what you're grateful for. Each night, record the top five things you are grateful for that day.

GRATITUDE JOURNAL DAY 1

1. _____

2. _____

3. _____

4. _____

5. _____

GRATITUDE JOURNAL DAY 2

1. _____

2. _____

3. _____

4. _____

5. _____

GRATITUDE JOURNAL DAY 3

1. _____

2. _____

3. _____

4. _____

5. _____

Gratitude Journal Day 4

1. ....
2. ....
3. ....
4. ....
5. ....

Gratitude Journal Day 5

1. ....
2. ....
3. ....
4. ....
5. ....

Gratitude Journal Day 6

1. ....
2. ....
3. ....
4. ....
5. ....

Gratitude Journal Day 7

1. ....

2. ....

3. ....

4. ....

5. ....

Gratitude Journal Day 8

1. ....

2. ....

3. ....

4. ....

5. ....

Gratitude Journal Day 9

1. ....

2. ....

3. ....

4. ....

5. ....

GRATITUDE JOURNAL DAY 10

1. _____

2. _____

3. _____

4. _____

5. _____

WAITING
FOR THE
CONSOLATION
READING: Luke 2:25–32

*Now there was a man in Jerusalem called Simeon,
who was righteous and devout. He was waiting
for the consolation of Israel, and the Holy Spirit
was on him. It had been revealed to him by the
Holy Spirit that he would not die before he had
seen the Lord's Messiah. Moved by the Spirit, he
went into the temple courts. When the parents
brought in the child Jesus to do for him what the
custom of the Law required, Simeon took him in
his arms and praised God, saying:*

*"Sovereign Lord, as you have promised,
    you may now dismiss your servant in peace.
For my eyes have seen your salvation,
    which you have prepared in the sight of all nations:
a light for revelation to the Gentiles,
    and the glory of your people Israel."*

Today, we're going to flip ahead a few scenes in Luke's Christmas narrative to the story of Simeon.

When we first meet Simeon, he's described as someone who's been "waiting for the consolation of Israel." He's been waiting his whole life for comfort. Something that will encourage his spirit and bring joy. This longing is for himself and his entire tribe, the nation of Israel.

For as long as Israel could remember, they had been ruled by one foreign empire after the next. Rome was just the latest in a long list. All of Israel was longing for the day when they would once again establish their own rule. They were waiting for God's long-promised Messiah who they believed would make that dream a reality. And, as we all know, the longer we wait, the harder it becomes to keep hope alive; the less faith you have that you will ever touch that which you long for.

At the time of Jesus's birth, Israel had been waiting hundreds of years for this Messiah. Chances are, there would have been some who had abandoned that hope completely. But Simeon hadn't. He was still waiting, despite how painful the waiting had become. His waiting was finally rewarded when he laid eyes on Jesus and felt able to die in peace.

In the bestselling book *Good to Great* by Jim Collins, we're introduced to the story of Jim Stockdale, a US military officer held captive for eight years during the Vietnam War. After he was released, Stockdale was asked how he kept hope alive during his imprisonment. His answer has famously become known as The Stockdale Paradox.[6]

"I never doubted not only that I would get out, but also that I would prevail in the end and turn the experience into the defining event of my life." While holding onto this belief, Stockdale also never put a timeframe on his release. He said those who refused to confront the dire reality of their situation were the ones who couldn't handle disappointment and didn't make it out alive.

"They were the ones who said, 'We're going to be out by Christmas.' And Christmas would come, and Christmas would go. Then they'd say, 'We're going to be out by Easter.' And Easter would come, and Easter would go. And then Thanksgiving, and then it would be Christmas again. And they died of a broken heart."

Collins sums up the Stockdale Paradox with this: "You must retain faith that you will prevail in the end, regardless of the difficulties. AND at the same time… You must confront the most brutal facts of your current reality."

---

6   See Jim Collins (2001). *Good to Great: Why Some Companies Make the Leap…and Others Don't.* Harper Business

Waiting for the fulfillment of all we dream and hope for can be painful. Especially if you find yourself waiting year after year, no closer to what you long for. The way to keep hope alive in your heart is to give space to all the longings that remain unfulfilled. You acknowledge all the anger, rage, disappointment, and despair your waiting has produced rather than letting it fester within. And you always trust that you will prevail, even if it takes a lifetime.

INVITATION

ALLOW YOURSELF PERMISSION TO
VOICE ALL THE ACHES AND GROANS
THAT LIE WITHIN YOU FROM
UNFULFILLED LONGINGS, TRUSTING
THAT YOU WILL ULTIMATELY FIND THAT
WHICH YOUR HEART LONGS FOR.

SPACE FOR REFLECTION

- What are the unfulfilled longings and dreams you are holding in your heart?

_____

_____

_____

_____

_____

- Where does your heart ache this Advent season?

_____

_____

_____

_____

_____

_____

Day
20

MAGI FROM THE EAST

READING: Matthew 2:1–8

After Jesus was born in Bethlehem in Judea, during the time of King Herod, Magi from the east came to Jerusalem and asked, "Where is the one who has been born king of the Jews? We saw his star when it rose and have come to worship him."

When King Herod heard this he was disturbed, and all Jerusalem with him. When he had called together all the people's chief priests and teachers of the law, he asked them where the Messiah was to be born. "In Bethlehem in Judea," they replied, "for this is what the prophet has written:

"'But you, Bethlehem, in the land of Judah,
*   are by no means least among the rulers of Judah;*
for out of you will come a ruler
*   who will shepherd my people Israel.'"*

Then Herod called the Magi secretly and found out from them the exact time the star had appeared. He sent them to Bethlehem and said, "Go and search carefully for the child. As soon as you find him, report to me, so that I too may go and worship him."

The story of the Magi is filled with mystery and intrigue. Who exactly are these strange travelers from the East? Why are they seeking Jesus? What does their presence at the manger represent?

First, it's important to note the phrase, "from the east." This makes the Magi outsiders in all ways: political, social, and religious. Being from the east communicates they're from another empire, specifically the Parthian empire (Persia). In the world at this time, Rome (West) and Persia (East) were involved in a series of conflicts over land. Neither empire wanted the other to encroach upon what they believed was theirs. By traveling from the East into the western Roman empire, the Magi would have been in enemy territory.

Once they arrive, they start asking for directions to the child born "King of the Jews." Not a great way to make friends when you show up looking to pay homage to some obscure child instead of the ones in power at the time. You've immediately targeted yourself as a political enemy.

Then, let's consider the religious aspect of the story. From ancient documents, we know the Magi would have advised the Persian kings about the will of the gods. They would have led some form of worship, making them priests. Magi were responsible for showing how the gods were at work in the world and leading others in that revelation. It is divine revelation that has brought them to Jerusalem, seeking where they believe their gods have led them.

When the Magi start asking for directions, the Jewish chief priests are called in. They search their scriptures, determine where the long-awaited Messiah is to be born, and the Magi are sent on their way to Bethlehem where they end up at the manger with Jesus. But who's not there? The Jewish priests. This is a scathing critique Matthew offers against the religious establishment. It's the Magi, religious outsiders, who find themselves correctly able to discern what God is up to, rather than the religious insiders.

Can we become so comfortable in a religious system that we end up missing where God is working? Can our religion become so self-consumed and inward-looking that we become blind to the work of the Spirit?

The story of the Magi can feel uncomfortable because it challenges our ideas about how God works. We like to feel in control of our religion and our understanding of God. But this story shows how the work of the Spirit is often a mystery that can't be contained in nice neat definitions. Instead, the Spirit is a dynamic force, using all means to reveal the hope of Christ being birthed in our world.

INVITATION

REFLECT ON ANY WAYS YOU'VE
CONFINED THE WORK OF THE SPIRIT.
TRUST THAT THE SPIRIT IS ALWAYS
AT WORK IN THE WORLD, EVEN IF IT'S
BEYOND WHAT FEELS FAMILIAR
OR COMFORTABLE.

Space for Reflection

- Have you ever experienced the Spirit in a way that went beyond your expectations of how the Spirit worked?

_____

_____

_____

_____

_____

- Do you ever find yourself controlling how and where the Spirit can work?

_____

_____

_____

_____

_____

_____

Day

21.

WHERE DID THAT STAR GO?

READING: Matthew 2:1–11

*After Jesus was born in Bethlehem in
Judea, during the time of King Herod, Magi from
the east came to Jerusalem and asked, "Where is the
one who has been born king of the Jews? We saw
his star when it rose and have come to worship
him."*

*When King Herod heard this he was disturbed,
and all Jerusalem with him. When he had called
together all the people's chief priests and teachers of
the law, he asked them where the Messiah was to
be born. "In Bethlehem in Judea," they replied,
"for this is what the prophet has written:*

"'But you, Bethlehem, in the land of Judah,
*   are by no means least among the rulers of Judah;*
for out of you will come a ruler
*   who will shepherd my people Israel.'"*

Then Herod called the Magi secretly and found
out from them the exact time the star had
appeared. He sent them to Bethlehem and said,
"Go and search carefully for the child. As soon as
you find him, report to me, so that I too may go
and worship him."

After they had heard the king, they went on their
way, and the star they had seen when it rose went
ahead of them until it stopped over the place where
the child was. When they saw the star, they were
overjoyed. On coming to the house, they saw the
child with his mother Mary, and they bowed
down and worshiped him. Then they opened their
treasures and presented him with gifts of gold,
frankincense and myrrh.

The Magi's journey would have taken months, if not
years. It was a journey hundreds of miles long with none
of the modern travel conveniences we take for granted.
The preparation alone for such a trip would have been
a massive undertaking.

Eventually, the Magi make it to Jerusalem, but there's a problem. The star they've been following has disappeared, leaving them lost in a foreign land. This is why they stop in Jerusalem to ask for directions.

It's easy to read this story and make certain assumptions.

First, we assume the Magi's time in Jerusalem was short lived. The story quickly flows from one scene to the next, but Matthew never reveals how long they were left directionless. How long did it take them to ask Herod for directions? How long did Herod keep them waiting before sending them on their way? We do the text a disservice when we assume everything was resolved in a night.

Second, we assume the Magi remained in good spirits their entire journey. Our nativity scenes depict three happy wise men offering their gifts to baby Jesus. Did their countenance remain the same as they witnessed the dimming of the star they'd been following for months? Did they experience despair? Would they have felt abandoned by their gods after traveling so far and not finding what they were searching for?

I'd like to think the Magi struggled with their faith like plenty of us. I'd like to imagine them sitting by their campfire at night, wondering what happened to the comforting presence of God they once felt. Reminiscing together about the certainty of their faith that has vanished along with their star.

The journey of the Magi parallels many of our religious journeys. In the beginning, we're filled with excitement. Everything feels new and nothing can take us off our path. Then, we have some experiences that don't quite fit our understanding of God, and we're left with a choice. We can either pack it up and go home, or rebuild our faith.

What inspires me most about the Magi's story is that, despite how they might have been feeling, they never gave up. They kept going.

This Christmas season, you may find yourself directionless. You've been following a star that's gone dark. The certainty you once held in your faith may have disappeared, leaving you disoriented, unsure how to move forward.

If you find yourself there, know that you are not alone. Others have traveled this road before you. The invitation is to keep going and trust that the same Spirit that brought you here will faithfully carry you forward. It may take a while. And it may require the restructuring of your faith, but your perseverance will be rewarded.

INVITATION

KEEP TRUSTING THAT GOD IS WITH YOU, EVEN IN YOUR MOMENTS OF LOSS AND DISORIENTATION. TRUST THIS EXPERIENCE IS AN OPPORTUNITY FOR YOUR FAITH TO DEEPEN.

SPACE FOR REFLECTION

- Have you ever experienced the loss of God? What did that experience feel like?

  _____

  _____

  _____

  _____

  _____

  _____

- Does it help to know others have experienced struggles with their faith?

  _____

  _____

  _____

  _____

  _____

  _____

Day

22

THE
ANXIETY OF
KING HEROD
READING: Matthew 2:1–16

After Jesus was born in Bethlehem in Judea, during the time of King Herod, Magi from the east came to Jerusalem and asked, "Where is the one who has been born king of the Jews? We saw his star when it rose and have come to worship him."

When King Herod heard this he was disturbed, and all Jerusalem with him. When he had called together all the people's chief priests and teachers of the law, he asked them where the Messiah was to be born. "In Bethlehem in Judea," they replied, "for this is what the prophet has written:

"'But you, Bethlehem, in the land of Judah,
*   are by no means least among the rulers of Judah;*
for out of you will come a ruler
*   who will shepherd my people Israel.'"*

Then Herod called the Magi secretly and found out from them the exact time the star had appeared. He sent them to Bethlehem and said, "Go and search carefully for the child. As soon as you find him, report to me, so that I too may go and worship him."

After they had heard the king, they went on their way, and the star they had seen when it rose went ahead of them until it stopped over the place where the child was. When they saw the star, they were overjoyed. On coming to the house, they saw the child with his mother Mary, and they bowed down and worshiped him. Then they opened their treasures and presented him with gifts of gold, frankincense and myrrh. And having been warned in a dream not to go back to Herod, they returned to their country by another route.

When they had gone, an angel of the Lord appeared to Joseph in a dream. "Get up," he said, "take the child and his mother and escape to Egypt. Stay there until I tell you, for Herod is going to search for the child to kill him."

So he got up, took the child and his mother during the night and left for Egypt, where he stayed until the death of Herod. And so was fulfilled what the Lord had said through the prophet: "Out of Egypt I called my son."

When Herod realized that he had been outwitted by the Magi, he was furious, and he gave orders to kill all the boys in Bethlehem and its vicinity who were two years old and under, in accordance with the time he had learned from the Magi.

King Herod's state of mind beautifully depicts how anxiety works. It starts within and flows from you, slowly engulfing all those in your path.

This word we read as "disturbed" in the above narrative is the Greek word "tarasso." Here are a few other ways to understand this word:

to agitate back and forth, shake to and fro

to set in motion what needs to remain still

to cause inward commotion; to take away calmness

Matthew is telling us Herod possesses no inner peace. His insides are torn up, and it's being felt by all those around him.

My guess is that this inner state is not something you aspire to. You're probably like me, desiring more serenity in your life. You've experienced that frazzled emotional state, and it's not pleasant.

It quickly becomes evident that Herod hasn't taken a master class on inner peace. As soon as his anxiety starts, he begins holding secret meetings. Instead of finding healthy ways to dispel his anxiety, he feeds it, and it only snowballs from there.

A few verses later, we're told Herod is furious for being outwitted and orders the death of all boys aged two and under (Matthew 2:16). The word translated as "furious" is the Greek word "thumoo." It indicates an outburst of passion and actions emerging from strong impulses. Herod is reactive, unable to control his behavior.

This all begins when Herod's way of life feels threatened. Magi show up on his doorstep, asking where the "King of the Jews" has been born. To Herod, this is a direct threat to his power and the life he's created for himself. "King of the Jews" is his title; now he has a rival.

We all have an idealized way we expect our lives to go. We work hard to achieve a certain life, and when something threatens that life, it's hard not to become agitated and scared of what we might lose. Our natural response is to grip tighter and fight to regain the control we feel slipping away. As we saw with Herod, this approach leads us further down the path of anxiety and reactivity.

There's a mantra I often repeat when I sense myself gripping something too tightly: "Let go." It was offered to me by a life coach I worked with. Whenever I find myself becoming stirred up within, I pause, take some deep breaths, and repeat a few times, "Let go." It's a gift I've used many times to recenter myself and calm my inner anxiety.

Some things in life are simply out of our control. Inner peace comes from recognizing what those things are and surrendering them to God. No matter how much we plot and scheme, the future is largely out of our control. Resisting that truth is futile. Better to surrender and let go, so we can face whatever comes our way with as much inner stillness as possible.

INVITATION

RECOGNIZE WHAT IS OUT OF YOUR CONTROL IN YOUR LIFE RIGHT NOW. SURRENDER THOSE THINGS TO GOD AND FOCUS ON BEING PRESENT TO WHAT IS WITHIN YOUR CONTROL AND ENJOYING THE ONE LIFE YOU'VE BEEN GIFTED WITH.

SPACE FOR REFLECTION

- Is there anything out of your control that you find yourself trying to control? Is this causing any anxiety?

_____

_____

_____

_____

_____

_____

- What can you let go of and surrender to God this season?

_____

_____

_____

_____

_____

_____

OPEN UP YOUR STOREHOUSE OF TREASURES!

READING: Matthew 2:9–11

After they had heard the king, they went on their way, and the star they had seen when it rose went ahead of them until it stopped over the place where the child was. When they saw the star, they were overjoyed. On coming to the house, they saw the child with his mother Mary, and they bowed down and worshiped him. Then they opened their treasures and presented him with gifts of gold, frankincense and myrrh.

By this time in the Christmas season, our tree has been fully decorated in our living room for weeks. Every morning, we'll plug in the lights and enjoy its beauty. But still, nothing beats Christmas morning with wrapped presents arranged beneath the tree. We get up, sit around the tree, and watch each other rip into the gifts we've hand-selected to give.

Part of the Christmas morning excitement is watching someone open your presents to them. You've thought about a gift they would enjoy. Sacrificed some of your hard-earned money. And when they're holding the wrapped present in their hands, you feel an anticipation as they remove the paper. Will they enjoy it as much as you're hoping they will?

When the Magi come to the end of their long and winding journey, this is what they do as soon as they arrive at the manger. After falling on their knees, they open "their treasures," presenting Jesus with their most prized possessions. I'm guessing their anticipation level would have been through the roof. This was the moment they'd traveled all this way for. This is the treasure they'd been carrying with them for hundreds of miles.

The original Greek word used for "treasures" goes far beyond physical possessions. It also includes "thoughts stored up in the heart and mind." These are your most treasured possessions as well as the wisdom you carry within. One definition refers to this being a "storehouse of treasures." I absolutely love that phrase. We all have our own "storehouse of treasures." And, just like the Magi, we have been invited to offer them to others. Our treasures are not only for us, they're to be gifted to the world in service.

It's important to note that the Magi gave from a place of joy. There was no sense of duty or obligation to give their treasures. Instead, they were overjoyed when the star reappeared and led them right to the place where Jesus lay. Their giving came from the overflowing of their heart. To them, it was pure joy to be in that moment, presenting the best of what they had.

The other day we looked at the joy announced by the angel to the shepherds in the field. It was a joy finding its origin in the grace of Christ. This same word is used by Matthew when he writes about the joy experienced by the Magi. This joy came from an awareness of the grace they'd received. And their giving flowed from that very same awareness.

Joyful giving begins with an awareness of grace. The favor, love, and joy of God is upon you. You've been gifted life. Breath. From this foundation, Advent invites us to open our storehouse of treasures and generously give our best to the world around us.

INVITATION

TAKE AN INVENTORY OF YOUR
"STOREHOUSE OF TREASURES." FIND WAYS
TO GENEROUSLY GIVE FROM YOUR
STOREHOUSE THIS CHRISTMAS SEASON.

SPACE FOR REFLECTION

- Make an inventory of your "storehouse of treasures."

  _____

  _____

  _____

  _____

  _____

- How can you generously give from your storehouse to those around you?

  _____

  _____

  _____

  _____

  _____

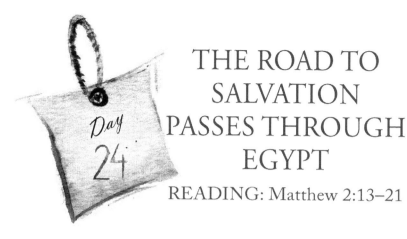

THE ROAD TO SALVATION PASSES THROUGH EGYPT

READING: Matthew 2:13–21

When they had gone, an angel of the Lord appeared to Joseph in a dream. "Get up," he said, "take the child and his mother and escape to Egypt. Stay there until I tell you, for Herod is going to search for the child to kill him."

So he got up, took the child and his mother during the night and left for Egypt, where he stayed until the death of Herod. And so was fulfilled what the Lord had said through the prophet: "Out of Egypt I called my son."

When Herod realized that he had been outwitted by the Magi, he was furious, and he gave orders to kill all the boys in Bethlehem and its vicinity who were two years old and under, in accordance

with the time he had learned from the Magi. Then
what was said through the prophet Jeremiah was
fulfilled:

"A voice is heard in Ramah,
*   weeping and great mourning,*
Rachel weeping for her children
*   and refusing to be comforted,*
*   because they are no more."*

After Herod died, an angel of the Lord appeared
in a dream to Joseph in Egypt and said, "Get up,
take the child and his mother and go to the land of
Israel, for those who were trying to take the child's
life are dead."

So he got up, took the child and his mother and
went to the land of Israel.

No sooner have the Magi left than Joseph is warned in a dream to leave Bethlehem for Egypt. Herod, feeling his power threatened, is searching for Jesus with the intent to kill. Joseph immediately flees with his family and Israel's promise of salvation is once again in doubt.

As we read about the flight to Egypt, we find ourselves in a world where Jesus, the long-awaited Savior, has been born, but nothing in the world appears to have changed. Deceit, violence, greed, and disregard for human life are on full display. And now, to further the blow, Jesus has been forced out of Israel by a power-hungry ruler.

This is a movement in the wrong direction.

The story wasn't supposed to go this way. God's Messiah was supposed to save us from sin, evil, violence, and despair, and now we're left wondering if those forces will be victorious in defeating God's plan.

Maybe you can relate.

For Matthew and the biblical writers, Egypt represents all that keeps us in bondage; all that holds us down, steals our hope, and prevents us from living in peace as the birth of Jesus promised.

We all have our Egypt.

We all have those areas in our lives where we struggle. Behaviors. Addictions. Crippling beliefs. Hopeless situations. No one is exempt. And the longer we spend in Egypt, the harder it becomes to hold on to hope and joy as we wonder if we'll ever be able to move past our struggles.

Matthew, knowing full well how deflating this flight to Egypt would have been for his readers, makes sure to let us know this has always been part of God's plan:

"And so was fulfilled what the Lord had said through the prophet: 'Out of Egypt I called my son.'"

Yes, you will experience struggles.

You will wonder if you'll ever be set free from that which enslaves you.

You will find yourself in situations that feel hopeless.

You will question when and if God's salvation will ever find you.

But don't give up hope.

Like Jesus, you have been called out of Egypt. You have been called out of the sin and the despair.

And, like Jesus, you will return home. No matter how long it may take, you won't be left in Egypt.

For Jesus, the road to salvation passed through Egypt. It's the same road we're all on.

What is your Egypt?

Where are those areas of struggle? The parts of yourself you wish you could move beyond?

The first step is to acknowledge the reality of your struggle. Acknowledge the power it has over you. And then surrender the struggle, trusting that God will be faithful to you. Trusting that, even as you tarry in Egypt, you have never been abandoned and divine love is with you, carrying you home.

INVITATION

ACKNOWLEDGE THE STRUGGLES YOU FACE. SURRENDER THEM TO GOD, AND IF YOU FEEL COMFORTABLE, BRING A TRUSTED FRIEND INTO THE STRUGGLE WITH YOU SO YOU DON'T HAVE TO FACE ALONE WHAT YOU'RE GOING THROUGH.

SPACE FOR REFLECTION

- What do you find yourself struggling with this season?

  _____

  _____

  _____

  _____

  _____

- Is there anyone you trust enough to share these struggles with?

  _____

  _____

  _____

  _____

  _____

Day
25

PONDERING IN YOUR HEART

READING: Luke 2:19

"But Mary treasured up all these things and pondered them in her heart."

We've come to the end of Advent! Today, we wake up at the moment our journey has been leading us toward.

In a few days, life will go back to normal. The celebrations will be over. Trees will be thrown to the street for woodchippers. The holiday lights and music will be turned off, and all the decorations will go back into their boxes until next year. Soon, it'll be life as usual.

Over these past twenty-five days, we've spent time slowly traveling through the story of Christmas. We've stopped at many places, peered into the lives of those we've met, and asked what invitations this story is offering for us today.

The question then becomes: How do we carry the spirit of Advent with us through the year? How do we protect the hope, peace, joy, and love we've received this season?

The story of Mary offers us the way forward. As the party at the manger is dying down, Luke tells us that Mary sneaks off behind the barn for some solitude. It's been a crazy time of activity with travel, giving birth, and one guest after another showing up to see her baby. Now she just wants to be alone. Just like her time preparing in the hill country, she needs space to reflect on all she's experienced. She needs silence to make sense of what's transpired and mine the wisdom she's gained through her journey. Mary also needs strength for the road ahead.

The same is true for us. Often, we don't see how far we've traveled or realize what we've learned until we stop and look back. We're used to movement and pushing ahead to the next step. But the wisdom being offered here is to stop. Like a lookout spot on the way to the top of a mountain, we need time to rest and contemplate where we've been.

As Advent comes to a close, I want to offer four questions for you to ponder in your heart:

- What has this season been teaching you?

- What new truths have you discovered in the story of Christmas?

- Where have you experienced God this season of Advent?

- How have you been changed through the birth of Jesus?

As you ponder all you've witnessed this Advent season, may you see all the treasures you've discovered along the way. May you see all the goodness of hope, peace, joy, and love the Spirit has birthed within you. And may that goodness carry you forward into this new year!

INVITATION

TAKE TIME TO REFLECT ON WHAT THIS ADVENT SEASON HAS BIRTHED WITHIN YOU.

SPACE FOR REFLECTION

- What has this season been teaching you?

  _____

  _____

  _____

- What new truths have you discovered in the story of Christmas?

  _____

  _____

  _____

- Where have you experienced God this season of Advent?

  _____

  _____

  _____

- How have you been changed through the birth of Jesus?

  _____

  _____

  _____

Keep in Touch

davestradling.com

Instagram: @dave_stradling

Sign-up for weekly emails full of inspiration,
my latest thoughts, and updates about my work:
davestradling.substack.com

Made in the USA
Middletown, DE
04 November 2023

41751054R00080